G000153753

Silent Voices

Silent Voices

*A selection of poems written
by those not always heard*

Not every disability is visable

Compiled and edited by
Jo Allmond and Joy Thomas

First Published in Great Britain in 2017 by Sandwords, Gloucestershire

Copyright © 2017 The contributors. All rights reserved.

The moral rights of the authors have been asserted

British Library Cataloguing-in-Publication Data
A catalogue record for this book is available from the British Library.

ISBN 978 0 9957408 0 8
E-BOOK ISBN 978 0 9957408 1 5

No part of this book shall be reproduced or transmitted in any form or by any means, electronic or mechanical, including photocopying, recording, or by any information retrieval system without written permission of the publisher.

Although every precaution has been taken in the preparation of this book, the publisher and author assume no responsibility for errors or omissions. Neither is any liability assumed for damages resulting from the use of this information contained herein.

Typeset in Goudy Old Style by Shepline Creative, Oxfordshire
creative.shepline.com

Contents

Writing about difference

How far should an author go? – with the approval of the disabled person, as far as is necessary within the boundaries of respect and sensitivity.

Is it ever right to come across as angry? – yes, at times it is necessary but in a controlled way, not just to vent your anger in an unreasonable manner.

How has writing helped? – it has helped enormously, it has given us and others a voice.

Everybody should have a chance to be heard, whether by speech, pictures, verse, music or movement.

We have endeavoured to give those people, who perhaps have never thought it possible, to put their thoughts, feelings and frustrations on paper for others to see.

It has been very emotional for us to read the work received and we feel privileged we have been allowed to include their work in this anthology.

Joy & Jo

Alone in the Playground

I was early as I walked up to the school gate.
There was a class playing in the playground.
I watched as children were laughing,
shouting, running and jumping.
Suddenly I was aware of a figure standing in the shadows.
A tiny, lonely figure, watching the others, my daughter.

She watched them with such longing, but couldn't join in.
Not strong or robust enough
she wasn't able to understand their games.
It was then I realised it was time to move on,
to find a place that would nurture her talents.
Though some couldn't see it, she had many.
I knew deep down it would be for the best
but I couldn't help feeling I was condemning
my child to a lifetime of limitations.
A life that would give her no future.
A life that would make her different.

I looked at my daughter
and watched with tears in my eyes

as the teacher gently took her hand
and led her into the classroom.
As she disappeared through the door
I did not know that I knew nothing.

Jo Allmond

A World of Silence

There's not a single noise,
No 'hush', no shout, no whisper,
Just silence, pure silence,
No roar of sea, wind or avalanche,
No rippling of waves against the shore,
No dripping tap, no raindrops on window pane,
No crackling of fire, shooting of sparks,
No whoosh of a firework rocket,
No flutter of a butterfly,
No rumble of a storm, no crash of thunder,
No ticking clock, no striking of the hour,
No howl of a wolf calling, no dog barking,
No call of a cuckoo, no dawn chorus,
No crunch of feet on gravel,
When you call, echoes fall back to me unheeded,
Like a barn owl approaching,
Life is silent, nothing else,
I am alone, why is there no sound?
Oh silence, do not mock me.

Annie Ellis

Alzheimer's

Do not ask me to remember.
Don't try to make me understand.
Let me rest and know you're there with me.
Kiss my cheek and hold my hand.

I'm confused beyond your concept.
I am sad and sick and lost.
All I know is that I need you
to be with me at all cost.

Do not lose your patience with me.
Do not scold or curse or cry.
I can't help the way I'm acting,
can't be different 'though I try.

Just remember that I need you,
that the best of me is gone.
Please don't fail to stand beside me.
Love me 'till my life is done.

Author unknown

Budget Day 2015

The deficits lower
George Osborne has said.
"Oh well" that's OK then,
he'll sleep sound in his bed.

Has he any idea
at what cost come his gains?
Does he know of the suffering?
Does he know of the pain?

What about Edith
who is stuck in her chair?
The people imprisoned
who don't go anywhere.

The centres are closed.
He's cut till we're bare.
No money, no future,
no staff left to care.

It's all about business
and financial gain.
Wheeling and dealing
and shifting the blame.

The fact we've paid into
the coffers for years

doesn't seem to hold muster
or dispel all our fears.

The books have to balance
of that there's no doubt.
But must you keep taking
from those who can't shout.

Carers in old age
don't get paid anyway.
I presume it's assumed
we don't need the pay.

Instead we keep going
in our role to care.
Trying our best
to do more than our share.

All that we ask
is to have a fair deal.
To have someone to be there.
To know needs are real.

It may be a burden.
Believe me I know.
It's not what we'd choose,
how we hoped life would go.

Whatever you say,
this country is rich.
There is no excuse,
no need for this gliche.

Pensions mis-managed,
money ill spent,
the vulnerable suffer,
in a system that's bent.

Don't make excuses,
they fall on deaf ears.
We've been there before,
we've been listening for years.

Joy Thomas

The steeper the mountain
The harder the climb
The better the view
From the finishing line.

Author unknown

Caring

Caring, not a job for all,
but for those of us who have the call.

A kindly look or a smile
to the lads would go a mile.

How much do they comprehend or understand?
For us to know, that would be grand.

We are there to help them make wise choices
not to put down with angry voices.

Perhaps we should help them and not be shy.
There but for the grace of God go I.

Would you be a mug
to give the lads a hug?

Perhaps this job just makes you meek
when one of them kisses you on the cheek.

Let's come to work with expectation
and leave behind any aggravation.

Neville Parsons

Caring

Caring is being there
when everything seems impossible
and the only memories remaining
are of times gone by.

Caring is having time
to listen when the mind
is confused and needs an explanation,
a reassurance that all is well.

Caring is having patience.
An understanding of the reason for changes,
the blank look and glazed eyes
as you retreat into your own world.

Caring is holding your hand,
accepting whatever you are,
and wherever you are,
I will be walking beside you.

Joy Thomas, 2016

Cast Off

Wool shunts through,
lightly grazes my hot fingers,
feeds unhurried growth.

Stitches are born,
they slip and loop, left to right.
The garment, a slow moving vehicle,
drives itself to clothe a small body.
Colours change at random,
spatter and daub their bright patterns.
The steady click relieves our silence.

You wake, touch the vibrant rows,
fingers icy and bloated.
"That's lovely", an arid whisper.
Your eyes close again,
the room too warm.
Voices drone through the door,
a distant buzzer calls,
the moon's thin slice glides through clouds.

The last piece finished,
I rest it on your cover
where it pulses gently with each breath.

Kathy Watson

Written in the hospice while knitting by her dying mother.

Kathy Watson lives in rural Shropshire. She has been writing poetry for about four years and is a keen member of a thriving local writing group.

Her brother is severely disabled, and since her Mum died, Kathy has taken a geographically distant but nevertheless significant role in his care.

Changing Direction

Worry can't cure desperation
Worry misuses imagination.
No fear keeps safe at night
Fear just fuels further fright.
Inhibition never delivers peace
Lack of it brings great release.

Imprisoning ourselves never sets us free
Shutting our eyes can't help us see.
It's not possible to just stand still
Immobilising destroys free will.
Kindness to others is only part
Kindness to self is truly smart.

Taking risks every day
We live fully when we play.
There are no must or ought or should
But only can and will and would.
Happiness comes from word plus deed
Fulfilment comes from meeting need.

Larry Gardiner

Crazy Horse

I'll tell you what a lot of
mental illness is about.
It's thinking bloody negative,
we fill our minds with doubt.

We fill our lives with pressure,
hassle, conflict, stress and pain.
We abuse our nervous system
the vicious circle's all the same.

We feel our very sanity is
teetering on the brink of no return.
A lot go through this time of hell,
but the lucky 'live and learn'.

Our negative emotions spin thoughts
spiralling inside our dizzy heads.
They reach to a crescendo
and we wish that we were dead.

We falter and we flounder
and cry tears of deep despair.
We're alone with all our conflict
and nobody seems to care.

This crazy, sweating, raging horse
is way out of control.

So very tightly pull the reigns
if you want to save your soul.

Harness this demented steed
Whisper softly in its ear,
and tell it not to be afraid
that it is only fear.

Speak gently to its beating heart
and fill its head with love.
Then lead it to a stable
and the peace of God above.

Gillian Gainsford Hodges, 2003

Written at a time when she had been a carer for her brother.

Dementia

I turn and feel your breath on my cheek.
So near, and yet a million miles away.
Fast asleep you look so peaceful.
Anxiety no longer etched on your face,
confusion resting till you wake from your slumber.

I try to imagine how you must feel,
remembering so much from long ago
yet not knowing who I am,
this person who sits holding your hand
whilst the sun goes down.

Sometimes I see a flicker, a glimmer of recognition.
You smile and I forget for a moment
just where we are
and that you don't know me.

Joy Thomas, 2016

Disabled

Scared, I'm different.
Nervous, who am I?
I don't know.
Angry.
We are the same,
but I am different.
I am disabled.

Jess Hiles

Encounter With a Stranger

Today I met a stranger
while travelling on the train.
We exchanged tales of laughter,
no mention of my brain.

They had no preconceptions,
no judgement had they made.
My dementia had lain dormant,
it behaved itself today.

I hope they saw the person
and not the disease in my brain.
I hope they thought me 'normal'
as we chatted on the train.

Our paths might never cross again.
About me they have no knowledge.
They took me at face value
Me, as a person. they acknowledged.

No disease was mentioned.
No hints of my decline.
No sign of my dementia
of that disease of mine.

Did they see me struggle
with the words inside my head.

Or clutching tight my suitcase
So as not to forget.

Today this person opposite
no judgement did they make,
no expectations crossed their mind,
no assumptions did they make.

For at the end of the journey
we went our separate ways.
During that brief encounter
I was just me once again.

Would they have thought or reacted differently

if they had known ... we'll never know.

Wendy Mitchell
Living as well as I can with dementia.

Five Hours

"Your daughter has a 50-50 chance."
Those words kept going round and round in my head.
"She is a very sick little girl."

Five hours we waited.
"Do you want us to call the priest?"
"Why, what can he do?"

If there was a God would he
put a little baby through this?
What had she done to deserve it?

Five hours we walked.
Did I do something wrong?
Was it my fault my little one was so ill?

Five hours we held hands.
We passed shops again and again
looking in the windows but seeing nothing.

Five hours we hardly spoke.
We didn't need to.
We knew what each other was thinking.

Five hours of hope. It was time to go back.
I'd watched my dad in tears,
mum take my son home.

I had watched them take our baby away,
her tiny body fighting to stay alive.
What were we going to find?

We walked through the doors
up to the empty cot,
and we waited.

The surgeon walked towards us.
What he was thinking I couldn't tell.
He stopped and looked at us.

"It went well, the operation went well.
There's a long way to go
but your little girl has pulled through.

She is going to live!"

Jo Allmond

Guilt

It never goes away
The guilt.
Was it my fault?
I am sure I did something wrong?
"Don't be silly" everyone says.
"Of course it wasn't you."

They don't understand.
I'm her Mum.
I saw her fight for her life.
I spent hours in hospital
willing her to live.
Feeling it was my fault, feeling the guilt.

I cringe when people stare and whisper.
There it is again, the guilt.
Why? Because she looks different that's why.
Was it something I did that made her different?
Why can't they turn away, walk away,
or even come and speak to us.

"It must be hard for you living so far away."
"No Jess knows I am always here for her."
"But you're not round the corner, so that must be
difficult."
Why is it? Stop it.
I can feel it creeping in again.
The guilt.

I try to shut it out.
Will it ever go away?
Am I ever to get peace of mind?
I don't know, all I do know
is I love her, I'm her Mum,
and I feel no guilt about that.

Jo Allmond

Hands Over My Ears.

There are days when I want to put
my hands over my ears and shout
in a loud voice "shut up", "just shut up."
It is incessant, the non-stop chattering
about nothing in particular, mainly
repetition of what was said yesterday.

Question after question, a cacophony
of sounds, regarding matters I have no
knowledge of and, in the normal course of events,
would not concern myself with.
I know, of course, I can't cover my ears,
hide under the duvet, or go around the world on vacation.

But the thought that I might, one day,
keeps me going, gives me some peace on
the most challenging, chattering days,
when I am a hair's breadth away from despair.
It leaves me with that little bit of hope
and stops me putting my hands over my ears.

JPM

If

If tears could burn
I'd still have a face.

If anger were let out
You couldn't see it in me.

If love became visible
I'd have no aura.

If hatred could kill
I wouldn't be here.

If confidence could glow
I'd live in the dark.

If fear was wet
Then I'd drown.

If loneliness were cold
Then I'd have hypothermia.

If self respect were solid
Then walk through me.

If willing were a wall
Then I'd be the exit.

If motivation were a cure
Then I'd be the disease.

If alcohol were the answer
Then I'd be the question.

Paul Staite

'My poems were an outlet for all the anger and hatred I suffered from due to being bullied all my childhood.'

'I am proud of the journey I have endured, I have come out the other side better.'

'Surviving my past has shaped who I am.'

A *flower*
does not
think of competing
with the flowers
next to it.
It just blooms

Author unknown

I'm Here, I'm Here

Sat in my wheelchair, in my mind I hear myself shout.
I'm here, I'm here and I want to go out.
My arm jerks out towards a staff member.
Not to hurt them, but for them to remember
I'm here, I'm here.

Oh! Look. A staff member who knows me well.
Thank goodness, I now know I am not in a living hell.
She gets down on her knees to be at my level
and touches my arm with warmth and compassion.
I'm here, I'm here.

"Have a good day?" I hear her ask.
I smile in response, because she makes me laugh.
My arm jerks towards her and I shout.
In response she says "let's get ready and we will go out."
I'm here, I'm here and I'm going out.

I'm here, I'm here, full of frustrations,
But staff who know me well
always give great interactions.
I am a nice person and will always smile.

You'll know that when you read
my communication profile.

Linda Powell

Isolation

He stands alone, facing the wall,
removing pieces of moss
that are growing in the mortar.
It's as though he is invisible, a nonentity.
The isolation is complete when the bell rings
and nobody calls his name
or notices he is missing.
He looks around the empty playground
eyes like saucers, staring, unseeing.

Loneliness envelopes his very being
shrouding him in a feeling of desolation.
All he wants is a friend, to belong, to be.
For someone to call his name and
acknowledge that he is, that he exists,
that he matters,
albeit in a world that makes no sense at all,
where nothing fits in or lines up quite straight,
and people say things they don't mean.

Like clouds having silver linings and
everything happens in threes.
He kicks the step with the toe of his shoe.

Everyone knows that clouds are white and
a visible mass of watery vapours
and that things just happen,
in any number, not just threes.

Joy Thomas
Taken from 'Slipped Through The Net'

I Asked The Little Boy
Who Cannot See

I asked the little boy who cannot see,
"What is colour like?"
"Green" said he "is like the rustle
when the wind blows through the forest;
running water, that is blue;
and red is like a trumpet sound;
pink is like the smell of roses;
and I think that purple must be like a
thunderstorm;
yellow is like something soft and warm;
and white is a pleasant stillness when you lie and
dream."

Anonymous

I Worry Mum

I worry Mum.
Do you love,
what about?
Everything, the world.

I worry Mum.
Yes, so you said.
How can I help?
Save the rainforest.

I worry Mum.
I know you do.
Must get tea, the girls will be back.
I want to adopt a tiger.

I worry Mum.
There's nothing for you to worry about.
But I can't stop.
I know love.

I worry Mum
You are going to give yourself a headache.
I know.
Try to relax and enjoy your tea.

I worry Mum.
It must be time for a bath.

White tigers are going to be extinct.
Let's talk about it upstairs.

I worry Mum.
Make sure that water's not too hot.
I want to join the World Wildlife Fund.
If you think that will help.

I worry Mum.
How can I stop you worrying?
Make my brain better.
Oh! My child, if only I could.

I worry Mum.
Let me tuck you up nice and warm.
I want to be normal.
I know you do.

I worry Mum.
What about now?
About everything.
I'll get you a warm drink.

I worry Mum.
Try and get some sleep.
I can't stop thinking.
I'll read you a story.

I worry Mum.
So do I love.
My brain won't stop.
Hush now, close your eyes and rest.

I worry Mum,
That's enough worrying for today.
But what will happen to the world?
Believe me son, it will just keep on turning.

Phillip Wynn & Joy Thomas, 1979
Taken from 'Slipped Through the Net'

Kindness

Never hurt, Never Harm
Always Gentle, Always Calm
Ignore the negative of your mind
Hold in your heart to just be kind
Love everyone no matter what
Hold a hand, give it all you've got.
Hurting people, love, is not
Stay positive, don't say 'forgot'
Open your heart always one more time
Keep on going, be it 'on the line'
Gentle with others no matter their display
It is only words they cannot say...
Know in your heart you are essentially good
And have a choice to do what you should.
Bless EVERY day, keep paying Forward;
Never hurt, Never Harm
Always gentle, Always Calm
Ignore the negative of your mind
Hold in your heart to just be kind
For even if, your heart's in tatters
Kindness always, ALWAYS Matters...

Em

Last Moment of Joy

Every moment, every pleasure
Every second, without measure
Every contact, every touch
Last moment of joy!

One day to live, one day to go.
Sunshine, wind and rain and snow.
Each breath is precious, one my last.
Last moment of joy.

Fill life with love, make it work.
Natures' gifts, wild and free.
Enough for you, enough from me
Last moment of joy.

Larry Gardiner

*I proclaim that people living with Cognitive Disorders
should have a right to a life worth living.*

Not a long slow undignified goodbye.

Leaving You

I stare at your face to see the love enshrined,
but glimmers of hope remain entwined.
You're shrouded in happiness and tears from the past
your troubles a burden too heavy a task.

As I witness your pain I strive to remain,
but all my attempts are to no avail.
Resolution has sprung, my dreams washed away,
as anguish and torment now roam and play.

My heart beats strong but my heads in a haze,
whilst I sit alone in this desolate place.
My brain is withered and our time now short.
Let's cherish each other till the day we part.

No time to miss no time to waste,
of the precious memories we both did make,
so come sit down and lets embrace
from dusk till dawn we shall recall.

My time has come I am lost in the haze.
I have no way out of my final maze.
My eyes do not sparkle, my heart does not sing,
our memories now consigned to oblivion

But know in my soul you will forever remain
guarded and cherished till we meet once again.

So don't be sad, smile through your tears.
Let the memories within have free reign

You will see my smile and remember my laugh.
The happiness you once knew again you shall have.
Your dreams will run wild and you will dance again,
as here by your side a loving angel I shall remain.

Anne Scott

*My thoughts on leaving my little daughter after being
diagnosed with dementia and multiple scleroses.*

Listen To Us!

Why don't people listen to us?
We want to talk.
Have a chance to speak.
Listen to us!

Say how we feel.
Nervous, anxious,
shy, confused.
Listen to us!

People talk over us,
Don't hear us, know how we feel,
what our thoughts are.
Listen to us!

If they don't listen
we don't feel valued,
understand it's rude.
Listen to us!

Karen, Debbie, Gill, Jess, and Frankie, January 2017
MacIntyre "My Voice" Redditch/Bromsgrove Group

Love You Mum

"Love you Mum!"
Comes from the room next door.
"You OK Mum?"
"Love you too Jess" I say with a smile on my face.

Jess, who has changed my life completely.
Who I wouldn't change for anything.

Except. Except what? Except I would change the world to
look at Jess for what she is, not what she isn't.

My Jess who loves everyone
and wants to be loved back.
My Jess who is so caring
and wants to help those
who aren't as able as she is.

My Jess who can walk into a room
and bring a smile to everyone's face she
says hello to, and make them love her.

"Love you Mum."

Jo Allmond

Meant To Be

I asked my dad.
"What would you do,
if your baby had Down's Syndrome
and you knew?"

He replied
"Well I'd support your mum,
but we'd probably abort
and try for another one."

I admired his ease
and his honesty
that baby could vanish,
it wasn't meant to be.

I guess I'm lucky
that my disability occurred at birth
and as a foetus
it didn't determine my worth.

Women have the choice
for that I'm glad
and I couldn't be closer
to my wonderful dad.

But if he had known
that I'd have a disability
would he have tried again
and aborted me?

Anonymous

Mum

Mum, where do you go?
My rock, my constant through the years,
I turned around and you had gone.
I look on your face now lined and wrinkled,
your once active hands lie still in your lap where I
would sit,
your eyes once full of love for me,
now empty of recognition.
Alzheimer's has you in its firm grasp,
pulling you, selfishly, closer day by day.
I can only watch,
powerless to return you to our world.

Celia Thompson

Celia Thompson's day job is in construction.
"I love arts and crafts and I now teach multimedia to
adults part time, a passion I inherited from my mother
who ran pottery classes for the blind before she contracted
Alzheimer's. "

Mum

Trying to say I'm sorry
is very hard to do.
Especially when I have a Mum
as understanding as you.

I know I can be difficult,
sometimes not honest or true.
What I'm trying to say is
that I really do love you.

You're always there for me
whether I'm up or down,
and you always greet me with a smile
never a scowl or frown.

Some mothers go over-the-top,
and spoil their 'little boys'
but I've always had to stand on my own
'cause you gave me the right toys.

Whenever I'm all mixed up
and luck seems out of sight,
I can rest in peace and rest assured
Mum'll be there to put it right.

And when I walk in upset,
and I think I'm in trouble
you always look sad and angry
but underneath you're full of bubble.

This is just a poem to show I care
I need to say I'm guilty, to apologise,
because what cuts me up
is the fear and hurt in your eyes.

Flower can't compensate
for all the wrong I have done,
but through this verse I can say...
"I've got the world's best Mum."

Paul Staite

My Brother

He is very tall.
Got a very hairy beard,
it tickles when I get a hug.

I like his tattoos,
don't like his earrings.
He goes to the pub
'cos he likes a beer,
then he talks too loud,
but he's lovely.

Sometimes I make him cross
when I text too much
but he buys me presents and cares a lot.

He's the best brother!

Jess Hiles

Pain

It's always there, this pain of mine.
Only sometimes not there,
but just around the corner.
Like a shadow it waits till you least expect.

One minute, or day, you think you are fine,
then all of a sudden it's
back with a bang, just making sure
you know it is there.

The pain, when it's bad causes me
to pain others, treating my family very badly indeed.
My pain, it is chronic, so with me forever,
but treatment is ongoing to blot out the pain.

I hope that it works to suppress my bad pain
as my life is on hold till I cleanse my mind.
I apologise to all my friends
                              if I am sharp and get angry.

It's not you that is causing it ...
                              It's my pain with no name.

Alan Allmond, 2016
Living with constant pain

People Watching

Lots of people
wearing coloured clothes.
Pushing prams.
Going home.

Couples holding hands.
People giving things,
some walking quickly,
some walking slowly,
some are running.
Going home.

People in wheelchairs.
People with guide dogs.
I like watching people
Going home.

Jess Hiles, September 2016

Phillip; My Brother

I can't remember the day I lost him.
I don't recall passing him by.
Once intimate soul siblings,
Bonds broke, I didn't know why.

My elder, my brother, my friend.
Known since the day I was born;
As we grew so did our differences,
I look back and try not to mourn.

He was taken from me, though returned,
later days in our adulthood.

Asperger's syndrome the thief,
the chasm I now understood.

My memories hold joy and happiness.
They also hold guilt and shame.
That I didn't glance back at my brother,
I didn't hear him call my name.

Mentally handicapped, brain damaged,
Hypoxic, labels, labels galore!
I wish I had waited and noticed,
I wish I had loved him more.

I fought for him in primary school,
I advocated his name to our dad.
But I let go his hand as I lived my life,
Not seeing he felt so sad.

How can he know he inspired me and
formed my choices by just being there,
can I ever make up for lost time?
Can I know that he knows that I care?

He has given much more than taken.
Filled my life at a level so deep;
I recognise now the blessing he is,
this is a love I will keep.

Bev, 2 August 2014
Poem from 'Slipped Through The Net'

Saying Goodbye

My journey will not be a long one.
I'm leaving it all behind.
But a long goodbye takes forever.
I'm slowly losing my mind.
There is no longer need to ever say sorry,
presence takes place in absentia.
The thing I forget is to worry
now I inhabit dementia
strip away all I aspire.
What I've lost I never grieve more
my brain packed it in to retire
marooned on some far distant shore.

Larry Gardiner

Smiling

Smiling is infectious,
you catch it like the flu.
When someone smiled at me today
I started smiling too.

I thought about that smile,
and realised it's worth.
A single smile, just like mine
could travel round the earth.

If you feel a smile beginning
don't leave it undetected.
Start an epidemic quick
and get the world infected.

Author unknown

So Tired

Today I am angry.
Yesterday I was weary.
Tomorrow I will be frustrated.
And always so tired.

No, you won't understand.
Not unless you have been there
or are there, living this nightmare
where you know what has to be done
but it never will get done.

The fight goes on
to give someone a life,
a quality of life they deserve.
A simple life where they
are no different from anyone else.

Frustration as yet another call comes.
Another fruitless meeting is demanded
where your voice is not heard.
You go round and round in circles
emotions rise until enough is enough.

I walk out, angry as I hit another brick wall.
I seem to have become a battering ram.
Nobody wants to listen because they

cannot or do not want to see the ways
that could make life so good for my daughter.

Weary, so very weary with constant worries, concerns,
and the one thought that never goes away.
It is there twenty four hours a day.
What if, what will happen, who will be there
for my daughter when I am not?

No one can give me an answer that will ease my
mind.
More importantly, that of hers.
I am just told "we will deal with it if it happens."
So tomorrow I will be frustrated, or angry, or weary
and always, but always, so tired.

Jo Allmond, September 2012

Take Me Back To 'Go'

Am I someone I know,
or just a copy of what I used to be?

Am I a mirror of my old self,
now pared down to the bone?

Am I still viable as a person,
or just a memory of what I once was?

Perhaps the memories I have
are only mirages of the mind.

More and more my brain takes me back to
childhood,
muddling the brain.

Semi remembered time and places
dance before me.

Is it now common for one to time travel?
Oh! Brave new world, please take me back to 'Go'

so I can have another chance at the muddle
that is my life.

Alison Bolus

Tormented

They can feel it digging
into their brain,
etching away
at the guilt that remains.

There's no chance of these people
being happy with their wives,
'cause they can't even live
with their tormented lives.

Hazardous thoughts bearing no name,
the pain is different, the guilt is the same.
Slowly they get older, older and emptier.
Still offering no escape from their secret fear.

Alone they are
no friends at all.
To suffer depression,
to walk empty halls.

So next time at a party,
whilst having fun,
spare a thought for the tormented
whose sorrows burn like the sun.

Please...

Paul Staite

Today

Today I'm glad I'm living
Today I'm feeling fine
Today dementia cannot beat me
Today dementia will toe my line.

Today I'll ignore the bad things
Today I'll be alright
Today I'll fight the challenges
Today I'll put up a fight.

Today I'm not thinking of tomorrow
Because Today I'm feeling fine.

Wendy Mitchell

Tubes

"You can hold her."
But I couldn't.
All I could see were tubes
like spaghetti junction travelling
round her little body.

"Really you can touch her."
But still I couldn't.
In case she would disappear,
sucked into one of those tubes,
those twenty-one tubes.

Suddenly a pair of piercing blue eyes
held my gaze.
From within those tubes
her eyes caught mine,
vivid deep, deep blue eyes.

I caught my breath and looked down.
A little hand was holding my finger,
clinging on from within those tubes.
I looked into the face of my daughter,
my tiny little girl, and smiled.

Jo Allmond

People can be mean
Don't take it personally.
It says nothing about you
But a lot about them.

The 'A' Thing

I was choosing apples when it started.
That familiar wail getting louder
and higher as it progressed.
I wanted to run, hide,
anything to avoid the memories,
even though this time it wasn't my child.

People stopped and stared,
tutting as they carried on with their shopping,
muttering under their breath.
To the uninitiated it must have seemed
close to murder at the very least,
and cruelty beyond belief.

"I'll be good, I'll be good mummy,
please let me have it. I promise I'll be good."
The very soul of the shop shook as the protests
became louder, more abusive and aggressive
and he started to hang on to trolleys and shelving
screaming at the top of his voice.

My heart went out to her, the mother.
She stood impassive, no show of emotion,
knowing any sign of weakness would be disastrous,
frightened to allow any feeling of shame
or anger to surface as her child clambered
over counters and produce.

I don't know your name,
and I will probably never see you again,
but I want you to know I felt for you today.
Knowing as I do this would only be one
of many such altercations,
I wanted to tell you that you deserve a medal.

Joy Thomas, 2016

The New Term

By Stockport, he needs his first pee.
My eyes flick to the poorly hidden glances,
to the gawping fascination of a child
as our Mum drags him backwards up the aisle,
her fists protrude his armpits.
His rigid calipered legs,
orthopaedic heels plough the British Rail carpet,
the twin grooves spoil the pile.
No-one offers to help.

My teenage shame and heat
pulse and fuse with the train's mantra
Cerebral Palsy, Cerebral Palsy...

Both seated again,
mum scowling and sweaty.
Abruptly, he remembers the journey's end,
the new school terms,
and without warning, slides
into a routine grief, issues his noisy bawl.
A dozen eyes snap on,
then off again,
find sudden interest through the grime
in the bleak, Cheshire landscape.
Cerebral Palsy, Cerebral Palsy...

A woman, kind and anxious,
offers sweets,
he yells his refusal, then emerges suddenly,
covered in snot, a big saliva grin.
Mopped dry now, bright eyes fixed on the paper bag,
he tries his new voice on the woman,
hard Salford vowels
now lengthened and softened
by the weight of his time in the South.
"They're not mints are they?"
Relief makes us laugh ourselves silly.

Kathy Watson
Written as a teenage sister of a brother with cerebral palsy

Why

Why do you stare at me?
I'm only a different shape.

Why do you glare at me?
My heart holds you no hate.

Why do you bully me?
I've done nothing wrong.

Why do you abuse me?
You hurt me all along.

Why do you hit me?
You make me cower in fright.

Why do you shout at me?
Now I won't go out at night.

Why do you ignore me?
You don't want to be my friend.

Why do you call names at me?
You drive me round the bend.

Why do you hate me?
Just because of the way I look.

Why don't you try to love me?
Please don't throw the book.

Annie Ellis, 23 March 2016

Thoughts For The Day

I am not here to change the world.
I am changing the world because I am here!

We are more alike than we are different.

Holding a grudge is letting
someone live rent free in your head.

Unknown

Take pride in how
far you have come
and
have faith in how far
you can go

Jo and Joy

Jo's professional working life began as a ballet dancer and has now taken her on to being an author. In between she has worked as a dance teacher, special needs assistant, Director of a theatre company for disabled/able young people, a driver and carer for the elderly with the Red Cross and working on a Helpline for a cancer charity.

But Jo's biggest achievements are her children. Tom, who has given her two gorgeous grandsons, and Jess, with whom she has published two stories in Jess the Goth Fairy books. They visit schools and spread the message 'It's ok to be different because we are all the same inside!'

Joy lives in Gloucestershire with husband Owen, collie dog Bonnie, and Maisie the rabbit.

Originally born in Lancashire she moved with her parents, in the 50's, to Northern Rhodesia. On their return to England they settled in Gloucestershire. She has three children, three step children, grandchildren and great grandchildren.

After retirement she was inspired to write about her experiences of life with Phillip, her son, who has Asperger's Syndrome and a learning disability.

She is passionate about vulnerable people and their families having a voice, and being able to make choices regarding their lives.

Unfortunately this is not always the case.

Acknowledgements

Our sincere thanks to all the authors who have kindly contributed to this publication.

They entrusted us to treat their work with sensitivity and respect and we hope we have achieved this goal.

Our aim is to raise awareness of those whose voices are rarely, if ever, heard, but need to be.

A special thank you to Thomas Shepherd for kindly donating his help and guidance in producing this book. Without his help the task would have been quite daunting, and have taken us much longer to finalise.

Last, but not least, thank you to our families and friends who have encouraged us along the way.

Lightning Source UK Ltd.
Milton Keynes UK
UKOW03f2254130417
299091UK00001B/19/P

9 780995 740808